This Book Belongs To

_____

and

I Love Me!

MY MIRROR AND ME

This book is lovingly dedicated to my Heartbeats:

Josiah the Great
Nyla Bear
Kyla HoneyBee

Love Buela

Anointed to Reign Publishers, located in the United States of America publishes this document. The information in this document is accurate and current to the best of the ability and knowledge of the author at the time of writing. The content of the document is subject to change without notice.

ISBN 10: 0-9741678-4-3
ISBN 13: 978-0974167848
Library of Congress Control Number: 2018941349

For author inquiries, readings, and speaking engagements, please contact:
Andrea R. Knight
(910) 401-3942
P.O. BOX 26679
Fayetteville, NC 28314

All Book Illustrations and Artwork: Dario L. Herrera, @IAm4Rio
Original Character Sketch: Kandara Parker

Anointed to Reign Publishers LLC.
www.A2RPublishers.com
P.O. Box 5591, Douglasville, Georgia 30135

My Mirror and Me

Written By:
Andrea R. Knight

Illustrated By:
Dario L . Herrera
Character Sketch By:
Kandara Parker

Anointed to Reign Publishers LLC.

Hi, my name is **Anjie!**

I am as **SMART**

as can be...

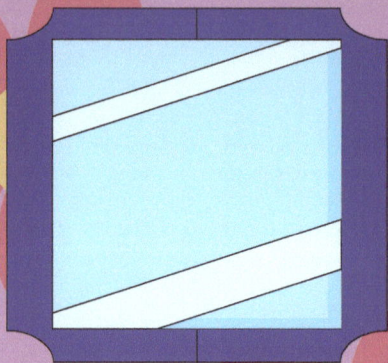

...And I love what I see when I look at **ME!!!**

My skin is brown,
but not like my dad's

And it's the
only skin I've
ever had.

I have three sisters, and even one brother!

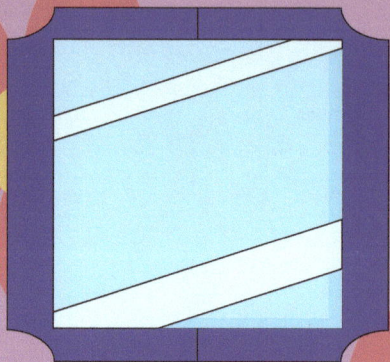

We all have brown skin some like dad's;

But mine is like my mother's.

A girl at church said I looked like a **clown**!

Said my skin was black so she wouldn't sit down.

I looked in the mirror and there was my skin,

I looked and looked and looked again.

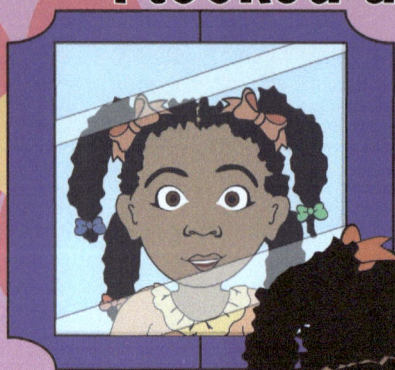

There was no clown or black to see.

I only saw brown beautiful ME!

My hair is black,
well it looks
   black to me.

It's black and
   curly as can be.

Mommy washes it
and combs
it and keeps
it clean,

But people can say
some really
   mean things.

05

Mrs. Lee said my hair is
dirty and nappy;

And that didn't make
me very happy.

I looked in the mirror
And there was
my hair

Neatly combed
with colorful hair
bows everywhere.

It was curly.
Not nappy and
clean as can be.

Mommy does a good job

And I love what I see!

My face is round and **perfect** as can be.

With a nose to smell

A mouth to speak and two bright eyes I use to see.

07

A boy at school laughed at my face; said I looked like an alien from outer space.

Said my eyes were big and my forehead too,

and I looked like a monkey out of a zoo.

I looked in the mirror and there was my face.

My forehead and eyes were in the right place.

They weren't big at all, well not big to **ME**.

I looked **perfect,** and no outer space alien did I see.

I looked like my grandma, and she's pretty too.

But I didn't see a monkey out of a zoo.

09

My arms are long, I use them a lot,

I catch butterflies, jump rope
and go swimming in
summer when it's hot.

I like to go to the park and play,
but the kids at the park were mean
to me today.

They said my
arms are way
too long,

said I can
play a solo
game of

Ping Pong.

I looked in the mirror and there were my arms; one on each side but not very long.

I use my arms in so many ways. I brush my teeth, comb my hair, and hug my mommy and daddy every day.

The game Ping Pong I would not play,

I never liked it anyway.

11

My legs are strong
and very straight;
I use them when
I jump, dance, and skate.

My legs can take me
round and round;

with skates on
sometimes
I fall down.

They move to the beat
of my **favorite**
songs.

They can dance a C jig all day long.

Ty says my legs are just too skinny;

Says they look like giraffe legs but not as **many.**

I looked in the **mirror** and there were my legs;

they're always moving is what mama says.

Left and right,
side to side;

A

I hold my head up
and move with pride.

My legs are
great and two
is plenty,

they're just the right
size and they're
not too skinny.

Giraffes have four legs and yes they are tall,

but I didn't see one in my mirror at all.

I have two hands and two feet, too;

and I can tell you what they do.

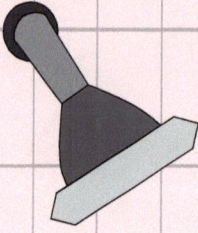

My hands they have
five fingers each,

and there are ten little
toes on my feet.

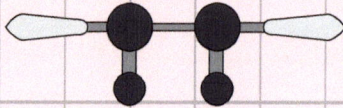

They clap, they stomp, and make
loud noise; fun things
to do for girls and for boys.

With my hands,
I play the flute and on my
feet I wear my boots.

Some Say my hands are big and my feet are long.

I clap my hands

while marching on, moving to my favorite song.

I really don't care what they say, it does not matter anyway.

17

I don't know what you see, but I **LOVE** what I see When I **LOOK** at **ME!**

A round face with two eyes, a nose, and a mouth to speak,

two arms, two legs, two hands, and two feet.

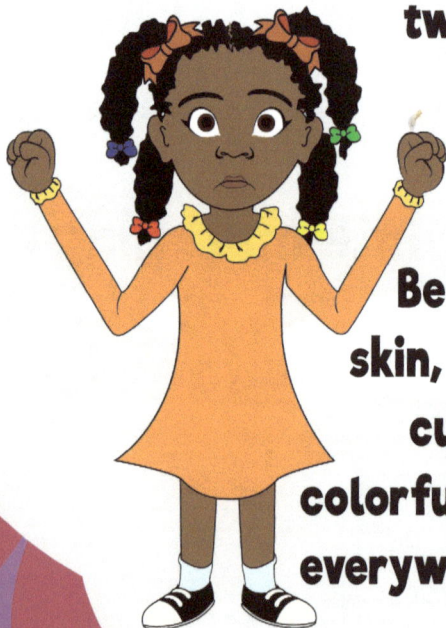

Beautiful brown skin, with black curly hair, with colorful hair bows everywhere!

When
I look
in my
mirror
I see
ME,

and that is
EXACTLY
who I want
to BE.

19

To My Friends:

Bullying is wrong and that is true,
You are the perfect, just right you!
Beautiful or handsome,
no matter what shade you are;
Believe in yourself, shine bright as any star!
People can be mean and say words that aren't kind,
Don't let it break you or change your mind.
Look in your mirror and smile at who you see,
Keep telling yourself...

I LOVE ME!

**To all moms, dads, teachers,
principals, and adult friends:**

Children are fragile and words are strong,
words can build a child up,
if they're not used wrong.
Your words can help and inspire me,
They can help me learn to be the best I can be.
When I look in my mirror please help me to see,
the beautiful person I was born to be.

ME!

Hi Friends,

It's me, Anjie! Every day and everywhere, people can say some really mean things. I call it bullying, and it can happen anywhere, at school, on the playground, at the park, at home, and even on the computer. If you see a friend being mean, ask them to stop, tell them it's not nice and that you don't like it! If they don't stop, tell an adult right away. Make a new friend today, I did, you are my new friend. Now, remember to be kind it's the right thing to do!

- Anjie

About the Author
Andrea Knight

Andrea Knight recognized and answered the call to her life's purpose early; as she has always been a protector of children especially little girls like Anjie.

Andrea has dedicated her education and career to working with children. Andrea's passion for children has led her to develop characters such as Mrs. Goofy to promote reading and literacy as she travels the country reading and telling stories to young audiences in libraries and schools.

My Mirror and Me is the first in a series of books to promote confidence and self-esteem in children, especially African-American children.

Andrea Knight has been married for over 34 years to her husband.

She is the mother of two children and she is a grandmother of three grandchildren.

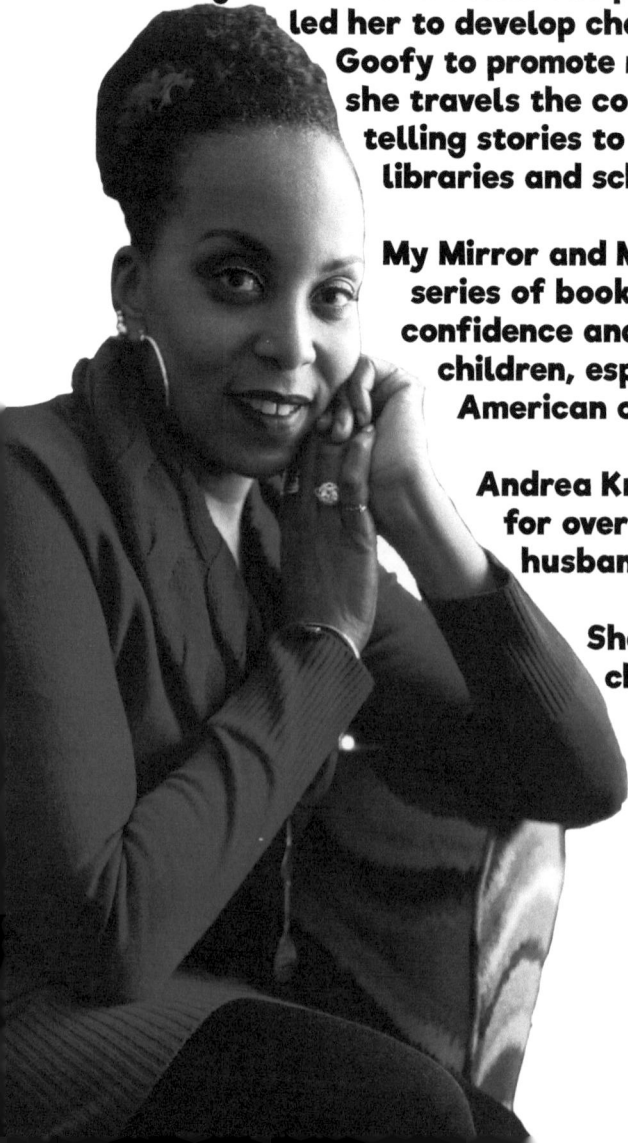

www.ingramcontent.com/pod-product-compliance
Lightning Source LLC
Chambersburg PA
CBHW041950110426
R18126100001B/R181261PG42743CBX00003B/1